Saint Bernadette Soubirous

Saint Bernadette Soubirous

And Our Lady of Lourdes

Written by
Anne Eileen Heffernan, FSP
and
Mary Elizabeth Tebo, FSP

Illustrated by
Mari Goering

Pauline
BOOKS & MEDIA
Boston

Library of Congress Cataloging-in-Publication Data

Heffernan, Eileen.

Saint Bernadette Soubirous : and Our Lady of Lourdes / written by Anne Eileen Heffernan and Mary Elizabeth Tebo ; illustrated by Mari Goering.

p. cm. — (Encounter the saints series ; 2)

Summary: A biography of the young French girl who lived during the latter part of the nineteenth century and who received apparitions of the Blessed Mother. Includes a description of Lourdes today.

ISBN 0-8198-7020-X (pbk.)

1. Bernadette, Saint, 1873–1897—Juvenile literature. 2. Christian saints—France Biography—Juvenile literature. [1. Bernadette, Saint, 1844—1879. 2. Saints 3. Women Biography.] I. Tebo, Mary Elizabeth. II. Goering, Mari, 1948– ill. III. Title. IV. Series.

BX4700.S65H45 1999

282'.092—dc21

[B]   99-18671
                                                                                              CIP

All rights reserved. No part of this book may be reproduced or transmitted in any form or by any means, electronic or mechanical, including photocopying, recording or by any information storage and retrieval system, without permission in writing from the publisher.

"P" and Pauline are registered trademarks of the Daughters of St. Paul.

Copyright © 1999, Daughters of St. Paul

Published by Pauline Books & Media, 50 Saint Pauls Avenue, Boston, MA 02130-3491. www.pauline.org.

Printed in the U.S.A.

TSBS VSAUSAPEOILL5-210061 7020-X

Pauline Books & Media is the publishing house of the Daughters of St. Paul, an international congregation of women religious serving the Church with the communications media.

8 9 10 11 12   20 19 18 17 16

Encounter the Saints Series

Blesseds Jacinta and Francisco Marto
Shepherds of Fatima

Blessed James Alberione
Media Apostle

Blessed Pier Giorgio Frassati
Journey to the Summit

Journeys with Mary
Apparitions of Our Lady

Saint Anthony of Padua
Fire and Light

Saint Andre Bessette
Miracles in Montreal

Saint Bernadette Soubirous
And Our Lady of Lourdes

Saint Catherine Labouré
And Our Lady of the Miraculous Medal

Saint Clare of Assisi
A Light for the World

Saint Elizabeth Ann Seton
Daughter of America

Saint Faustina Kowalska
Messenger of Mercy

Saint Francis of Assisi
Gentle Revolutionary

Saint Gianna Beretta Molla
The Gift of Life

Saint Ignatius of Loyola
For the Greater Glory of God

Saint Joan of Arc
God's Soldier

Saint John Paul II
Be Not Afraid

Saint Kateri Tekakwitha
Courageous Faith

Saint Martin de Porres
Humble Healer

Saint Maximilian Kolbe
Mary's Knight

Saint Pio of Pietrelcina
Rich in Love

Saint Teresa of Avila
Joyful in the Lord

Saint Thérèse of Lisieux
The Way of Love

Saint Thomas Aquinas
Missionary of Truth

Saint Thomas More
Courage, Conscience, and the King

*For even more titles in the
Encounter the Saints series,
visit: www.paulinestore.org.*

Contents

1. Poor and Small 13
2. The Wonderful Day 17
3. A Fantastic Story 25
4. More Excitement 29
5. Promises 35
6. Three More Apparitions 41
7. Interrogation 45
8. A Mysterious Force 51
9. The Miraculous Spring 57
10. Another Summons 63
11. The Request 67
12. The Chapel and the Pastor 71
13. Annunciation Day 81

14. A Temporary Farewell 87

15. Decision 93

16. Still Poor and Small 97

17. Lourdes Today 107

Prayer 111

Glossary 112

1
POOR AND SMALL

A baby's loud wails pierced the quiet of the church that January 9 in 1844. Two-day-old Bernadette Soubirous squirmed and kicked as the cold baptismal water was poured over her head. "All she does is cry," her embarrassed godfather mumbled.

"Nonsense!" snapped Bernadette's aunt and godmother, Bernarde Castérot. "She's a sweet little girl," she insisted, smiling down at the infant who had been named in her honor.

Bernadette's parents, Louise and François Soubirous, would have nine children altogether. Only Bernadette, Toinette, Jean-Marie and Bernard-Pierre would reach adulthood. Four other sons and another daughter died young.

The Soubirous family was poor. For several years they lived in an old mill—the Boly Mill—in the village of Lourdes, France.

One day a heavy knock on the door announced a visitor. Mrs. Soubirous answered it to find the mill's owner standing there. "Is your husband home?" he asked, nervously twisting the beret he held in his hands.

"Yes. Yes, please come in," she invited, and then called, "François! You have a visitor."

"I'm coming," a voice answered from the back room.

The landlord got right to the point. "François, I know you have a big heart, but if you don't collect the debts that people owe you, how can you ever expect to pay your rent?" Again the hat twisted in his hands. "I'm afraid you and your family will have to move."

"But where will we go?" Mr. Soubirous gasped in panic.

"I don't know. I'm sorry," the landlord sighed. "All I know is you can't stay here any longer."

A few days later, as the family quietly trudged down the dirt road leading from the mill, a voice cried, "Wait!" Mr. and Mrs. Soubirous turned to see André Sajous, Mr. Soubirous' cousin, running after them. "You can come and live at my house," he told them. "It's not much, but at least it will be a roof over your heads."

The "house" turned out to be an old prison. And the Soubirous family would live downstairs, in the darker, dungeon-like room, for a long, dreary year.

The family tried to make the best of their dingy, one-room home. But sometimes Mrs. Soubirous got discouraged. "I try to make things more comfortable," she tearfully protested one day, "but how much can I do with just three beds and a chair?"

"Dry your tears now, Louise," her husband comforted. "The good Lord must have something better in mind for us. He must."

The dark and damp environment wasn't a good one, even for a healthy person. But it was especially hard on Bernadette. When she was six, Bernadette had come down with cholera. Later she had also developed asthma and stomach problems. Because of her asthma, which already made breathing a struggle, the room's thick air was often unbearable. At times she would stand by the one barred window, gulping great breaths of the fresh, clean air which blew down from the Pyrenees Mountains. When she was having an especially bad asthma attack, she'd go upstairs to the Sajous' quarters where the window was bigger and let in more of a breeze. At night she couldn't do this without disturbing the family. She spent many sleepless hours lying next to her sister Toinette, suffering as silently as possible and trying not to cough. For all her life Bernadette would remain very small and frail.

That same asthma kept Bernadette from attending school and catechism classes regularly. Instead, she spent most of her time helping her mother and taking care of her younger brothers. Already fourteen years old, Bernadette was behind many of the younger students at school. A friend of the family tried to teach her catechism, but Bernadette's memory wasn't very good, and she never remembered the answers. One day the woman cried out in exasperation, "Bernadette, you're just ignorant, and you always will be!"

"You're right!" Bernadette replied, giving the woman a hug, "but I know how to say my rosary and I do love the good God with all my heart!"

Bernadette tried not to show how much her "thick-headedness," as she called it, bothered her. She only let herself cry about it when no one else was around.

2
THE WONDERFUL DAY

Thursday, February 11, 1858, dawned cold and misty. The fire was going out and the chilly room seemed darker and damper than ever. Bernadette walked over to the hearth. "Mama, where's the wood you and Toinette collected yesterday?"

"We had to sell it to buy some bread," Mama Louise sighed sadly.

Toinette was gazing distractedly out the window. "Look! Here comes Jeanne Baloume! ("Baloume" was Jeanne's nickname because she was big and strong for her age.) She'll come with Bernadette and me to get more wood."

Bernadette looked hopefully at her mother.

"It's drizzling outside, Bernadette," Mrs. Soubirous objected. "You shouldn't go. Your cough might come back again."

"Please, Mama," Bernadette begged, "let me go. I'll wear my cloak and hood so I don't get cold."

Mama Louise sighed again. "All right,

since you really want to. But make sure you don't get your feet wet!"

"I won't. I promise!" Bernadette laughed as she hurriedly slipped on her sabots, a pair of wooden clogs. Toinette and Jeanne were already out the door.

It didn't take very long to reach the Gave River. In the foggy mist the girls made out a bent figure washing something. As they came closer they recognized a familiar, wrinkled face.

"Mrs. Pigoune, what are you doing out in this bad weather?" Jeanne asked.

"I'm cleaning parts of the pig Mr. Clarens just butchered. And what are you girls up to?"

"We're looking for firewood."

"Well, then, keep to your right and go toward Massabielle," the peasant woman directed. "You'll find plenty of wood there."

"Thank you!" the girls called as they started out again. They had never explored that area before. It would be fun.

They soon reached the cliff of Massabielle. At its base was a grotto, a kind of natural cave carved out of the rock. All around the grotto the girls could see quite a bit of firewood scattered here and there on the ground. The problem was that a small stream, branching off from the Gave River, separated them from the grotto and the wood. But nothing was going to stop Jeanne. She enthusiastically kicked off her sabots. Throwing them across the narrowest part of the shallow stream, she started to wade through the icy water. "Come on, Toinette," she giggled. "It's not that bad!"

Toinette, following Jeanne's example, hopped into the water, squealing loudly. Once they reached the other side, the girls frantically rubbed their numb feet with their long skirts. Bernadette stood watching. Her mother's warning still echoed in her ears, "Don't get your feet wet!"

"Toinette!" called Bernadette. "Help me throw some big stones in the water so I can walk across."

"Maybe I could carry you," Toinette shouted back.

"No. You're too small," Bernadette countered. "I think Jeanne could do it."

But Jeanne wasn't too happy that Bernadette had come along in the first place. "You're such a nuisance, Bernadette!" she yelled. "Just stay where you are if you can't cross over."

As the bells of Saint Peter's Church pealed out the Angelus, and its echoes died away among the hills, Jeanne and Toinette, skipping to keep warm, quickly gathered the pieces of wood which lay near the grotto. Then they moved farther off to search for more. Bernadette was left alone.

At first, she tried throwing stepping stones into the stream, but the attempt failed. Next she decided to take off her stockings and sabots and wade over as the others had done. Just then, she thought she heard a rumble of distant thunder—or was it a sudden gust of wind? Bernadette glanced behind her. There were no storm clouds. None of the trees were moving. *It's nothing*, she thought as she began pulling off her other stocking.

But there was the same sound again! This time Bernadette stood up and carefully looked around in every direction. Suddenly her eyes were drawn to a spot above the grotto, another smaller hollow in the cliff where a wild rosebush was tossing violently, as if caught in a gale. Everything else was perfectly still.

As Bernadette stared at the bush, she saw something behind it! The hollow seemed to be filling with light. In the midst of the light appeared a beautiful young lady dressed in white. Bernadette watched in amazement as the lady came forward to the edge of the opening in the rock and stood right above the rosebush. She gazed down on Bernadette with a warm, welcoming smile, and motioned her to come closer.

Bernadette felt numb. She rubbed her eyes, shut them tight and opened them again. The lady was still there.

Hardly knowing what she was doing, Bernadette reached into her apron pocket and pulled out her rosary. She knelt down. But when she tried to make the sign of the cross, she couldn't raise her hand to her forehead. A shiver of fear ran through the girl. *What was happening?* As Bernadette watched, the young woman slowly and reverently made the sign of the cross. Bernadette tried again to bless herself. This time she was successful. As she made the sign of the cross, all her fear melted away.

Bernadette began to pray the rosary. The lady was holding a rosary but she passed its beads through her fingers without speaking or moving her lips. She silently moved her lips only during the "Glory be to the Father, and to the Son, and to the Holy Spirit...." at the end of each mystery.

She's very young, Bernadette was thinking as she continued to gaze at the lady. *Maybe only sixteen or seventeen, but so beautiful!*

Every detail was impressing itself on Bernadette's memory. She would later describe the long white dress which was closed at the neck and hung to the lady's feet, and the white veil which covered her head and shoulders and almost reached the ground behind her. A blue sash encircled her waist. She held a rosary of large, white beads spaced far apart on a gold chain. Two yellow roses rested on her bare feet. She was surrounded by light.

When Bernadette had finished praying the rosary, the young lady smiled and moved back into the niche in the cliff. In a moment or two she had disappeared, and the bright light had faded away. All was as it had been before. All except Bernadette.

Jeanne and Toinette, returning on the opposite side of the stream, were annoyed when they saw Bernadette right where they had left her—and on her knees besides!

"All she knows how to do is pray," complained Toinette.

"You could at least help us," Jeanne called sarcastically.

Bernadette nodded. She immediately pulled off her second stocking, stepped into the stream, and waded across. The water felt warm. "Why did you tell me the water was cold?" she said as she pulled her stockings and sabots back on. "It wasn't cold at all!"

By now Toinette and Jeanne were getting aggravated. But when they realized that Bernadette wasn't joking about the warm water, they were amazed.

Jumping up, Bernadette quickly collected a pile of branches and tied it in a bundle. She plopped it down by her sister's armload. "Did you see anything at the grotto, Toinette?" she asked cautiously.

"No. Why?"

"I was just wondering, that's all.... It's getting late. We'd better start back."

Impatient Jeanne ran on ahead, while the two sisters walked together. Toinette was burning with curiosity. "What did you see back there?" she prodded. Bernadette shifted her bundle and kept on walking.

"I'll keep it a secret, I promise," Toinette whined.

"You really promise?"

"Yes!"

The words came tumbling out and in a

few minutes Bernadette had told her sister everything. At first, eleven-year-old Toinette was scared. But soon enough her fear changed to anger and jealousy. *Who does Bernadette think she is, anyway?* she thought to herself. *She's always getting special treatment...stockings to wear, better bread to eat. Now she's making things up!*

Toinette had to find a way to tell this strange story to Mama. She just had to.

3

A Fantastic Story

"Ouch! It's pulling!" Toinette moaned.

"Well, if you'd keep still this job would be much easier," Mrs. Soubirous chided as she ran the comb through Toinette's thick hair. "I know you worked hard gathering that wood in the forest, but you don't want to be going around with bits of leaves and things stuck in your hair, now do you?"

Toinette didn't answer. She was planning her strategy. *If Mama asks me what happened today, I'll have to tell her. That won't be breaking my promise.*

Toinette started coughing and clearing her throat. She kept it up.

"What's wrong?" her mother finally asked.

"Nothing. I was just thinking about what happened today."

"And what was that?"

"Bernadette saw a lady in the rocks at Massabielle!"

"A lady? In that wild spot? Who was it, Bernadette?"

Louise Soubirous' face grew very serious as she listened. She had never heard her sensible eldest daughter tell such a fantastic story! "You must get these ideas out of your head at once," she insisted. "And don't go back there again!"

Mama Louise's decisions never changed. Bernadette hung her head. That night at the supper table everyone ate their watery soup without a word. Bernadette started to cry during evening prayers.

Mrs. Soubirous needed some good advice. She slipped upstairs after supper and knocked on the door of the Sajous' house. Romaine Sajous had five children. She might know what to do.

"Romaine," Mrs. Soubirous called softly, "I need to talk to you!"

Mrs. Sajous pulled open the door. "What's wrong, Louise?" she asked in alarm. "You look so worried."

"It's Bernadette..." Mrs. Soubirous began. When she had finished, Mrs. Sajous shook her head. "I'll come downstairs with you now and talk to Bernadette myself. My advice is give her a little more work to do. That should put an end to these daydreams."

Mrs. Soubirous was relieved as the two women headed back down the rickety stairs. Maybe Romaine was right. She hoped so.

After all the lectures and questioning, Bernadette didn't sleep that night. She tried to believe that she hadn't seen anyone—as her mother had said. But she knew deep in her heart that she *had* seen the lady. And she just couldn't get her out of her mind. If only she could see her again!

The next day word spread quickly that Bernadette Soubirous had seen a mysterious lady at the grotto.

The townspeople shook their heads in pity: "She's crazy, poor child."

Some laughed. The rest paid no attention. "This talk will die down soon enough," they muttered, going on to turn their gossip in other directions.

Bernadette felt as if a gentle but firm hand were pushing her toward Massabielle again. Usually very cheerful, the girl now appeared serious and thoughtful. Her mother couldn't help noticing the change and adopted a gentler tone of voice. "Believing in such strange things is dangerous, Bernadette," she warned. "What if it's the devil trying to trick you?"

"But Mama, the devil would never say the rosary," Bernadette quietly replied. "And he could never be that pretty, either!"

Louise was worried. Her teenager had never been so hard to convince.

4

MORE EXCITEMENT

Bernadette had met the lady on a Thursday. By Saturday, she felt so strongly drawn to the grotto that she began begging her mother to let her go again. By Sunday, the urge to return to Massabeille was overpowering. But Bernadette had given up asking. She stood in the background, her eyes silently pleading, while Toinette and Jeanne stormed her mother with protests. They were curious about what had happened at the grotto. They just had to go back and investigate.

Mrs. Soubirous finally gave in, "You may go if your father gives you permission," she said wearily.

Mr. Soubirous was working at a nearby stable when Bernadette, Toinette, Jeanne, and some of their friends came to beg his permission. "No!" was his stern answer. But his boss saw it differently. "Ah, François, what harm can a young lady with a rosary do? Let the children go to Massabielle."

"All right. Go if you must, but be back in

time for Vespers," Mr. Soubirous said gruffly.

One of the girls suggested taking some holy water. They could sprinkle it on the lady to make sure that she came from God and not from the devil. It seemed like a good idea. Armed with the holy water, the little group set out.

"Isn't Jeanne coming?" someone asked as they headed toward the river.

"She was going to," someone else replied, "but if we wait for everybody, we won't get back in time for Vespers."

At Massabielle, Bernadette fell to her knees exactly where she had knelt the first day. "She's there! She's there!" she exclaimed.

"Quick, quick! Throw the water!" One of the girls handed the bottle to Bernadette, who threw some of the holy water toward the cleft in the rock. "If you come from God, come forward!" she said. The smiling lady obligingly moved up to the very edge of the niche!

The others, who saw nothing, now knelt down near Bernadette. They looked from her to the hollow in the cliff and back again. They couldn't understand what was going on.

Bernadette's peaceful gaze was fixed on

the hollow space behind the rosebush, and her face had taken on such a heavenly expression that the girls thought she must be dying. As the seconds slipped by, their tension mounted. Suddenly, something came crashing down the slope above and splashed into the Gave! The girls jumped to their feet in panic.

"It's only a rock!" someone shouted. But no one listened. Everyone was screaming and running—everyone, that is, except Bernadette.

A short distance away, the fleeing girls met Jeanne, who had pushed a heavy rock down from the top of the cliff as a practical joke.

Calmer now, the friends made their way back to the grotto, where they found Bernadette in the same position. She didn't seem to hear them at all and when they tried to get her to stand up, they couldn't budge her. Her bright expression and fixed gaze gave them an eerie feeling.

"She must be dying," whispered one.

"I'm scared," whimpered another.

"So am I. Let's get out of here!"

"Wait! We can't just leave her here. Let's get Antoine Nicolau, the miller. He's strong. He can carry Bernadette home."

Young Antoine soon arrived on the scene with his mother. What all the nonsense was about he had no idea. He felt like giving the girls a good piece of his mind, but at the sight of Bernadette he stopped short. He had never seen anything like the expression on her face. With difficulty, but great gentleness, he lifted Bernadette to her feet and half carried, half led her to his mill.

Wide and unblinking, Bernadette's eyes stared at Something ahead of her, which seemed to keep pace with Antoine's strong steps. In vain the miller tried to break her trance: he put his hands over her eyes; he bent her head downward. But always Bernadette's head returned to the same position, and her eyes gazed steadily at...who knew what?

When they reached the mill, Bernadette finally blinked and looked around.

"Tell us what happened," urged the miller's mother.

Bernadette told them about the beautiful lady who had smiled at her and moved her own rosary beads through her fingers as the girl prayed. The young lady had moved her lips only at the end of each decade, and had disappeared in silence.

Meanwhile, Bernadette's friends were running back to Lourdes in groups of two's and three's. Poor Toinette was so overwhelmed that by the time she reached home she couldn't speak. Her shoulders heaved in great sobs.

"Toinette, what's wrong?" her mother asked in alarm. When Toinette only gestured toward the river, Mrs. Soubirous rushed from the house and began to run toward Massabielle.

"Where's Bernadette?" she cried to a small group of girls coming from the direction of the river.

"At Antoine Nicolau's house," one of them replied. Mrs. Soubirous' fear turned to rage. Now that she knew Bernadette was all right, she was furious with her for begging to go to the grotto, and furious with herself for having granted permission!

Bursting in upon Bernadette and the anxious group clustered about her, the mother began to scold her, "So, you'd make us the laughingstock of the town, you with your holy ways and stories of mysterious ladies!"

She had drawn her hand back to deal her eldest a slap on the ear, when someone grasped her arm. Looking down, Mrs. Soubirous saw the firm and gentle hand of Antoine's mother. "What are you doing?" asked the older woman. "Why should you strike your daughter when she is an angel from heaven?" While Louise stared at her in astonishment, the woman added, "I'll never forget what I saw today at Massabielle."

"A girl like this should not even be touched," agreed Antoine.

Suddenly Mrs. Soubirous felt very weak. She sank into a chair. Her eyes began to fill with tears.

A few minutes later she set out for home hand-in-hand with Bernadette. As they walked, the teenager kept glancing back over her shoulder toward the grotto of Massabielle.

5

Promises

Lourdes was soon humming with news of the young lady's second appearance. Groups gathered outside the Soubirous' shabby home to ask Bernadette and the other members of her family about the events at the grotto. Bernadette told them everything.

Some people were already speculating about who the strange lady might be. The devil? A soul from purgatory? The Blessed Mother herself?

Mr. and Mrs. Soubirous were afraid. They were sure that something evil was going on at Massabielle. "You're not to go to Massabielle again, Bernadette," they ordered.

Yet a mysterious, irresistible force was pushing the girl toward the grotto. By Wednesday evening, she was begging for permission to return, and her mother was once again saying, "No."

Help arrived unexpectedly. A young woman named Antoinette Peyret and a wealthy widow named Madame Milhet asked to go to the grotto with Bernadette. Since Mrs. Soubirous sometimes worked for Madame Milhet, she felt she had to give in to the request and allow Bernadette to accompany the ladies.

Very early on Thursday morning, while Lourdes was still cloaked in silence, Bernadette and her companions assisted at Mass and made their way to Massabielle. So eager was Bernadette to see the young lady, that she reached the grotto first, in spite of her difficulty in breathing. When the others caught up, she was already kneeling, her rosary in her hands, gazing toward the hollow in the rock. After a moment, she exclaimed, "Oh, how beautiful she is!"

Antoinette took a blessed candle she had brought with her and propped it up against a stone. She and Madame Milhet knelt down near Bernadette and began to pray the rosary too. At the end of the rosary, Antoinette took out paper, pen and ink, and handed them to Bernadette. "Ask the lady if she would please write down her name for us," she directed.

Obediently, Bernadette rose to her feet and approached the opening in the rock. Her companions followed.

But something strange was happening! The lady was stepping backward. "Please move farther away," Bernadette urged Antoinette and Madame Milhet. They moved back at once.

The young lady returned to the edge of the niche and Bernadette respectfully held out the paper, pen and ink bottle: "Would you please write down your name and what you wish?"

The lady laughed good-naturedly and then spoke to Bernadette for the first time, "It is not necessary for me to write what I wish to tell you," she said in a soft voice. "Will you do me the favor of coming here for fifteen days?"

"Yes!" Bernadette replied joyfully.

The young lady went on, "I do not promise to make you happy in this world, but in the next."

With a gesture of profound respect, Bernadette returned to the rock where she had knelt before. She gazed at the beautiful, smiling lady, and, after a moment or two, told Antoinette, "The lady is looking at you right now."

Gathering up her courage, Antoinette asked, "What did she say? May we come here with you again?" Bernadette ap-

*"Would you please write down
your name and what you wish?"*

proached the grotto a second time. In a moment she relayed the reply: "Yes."

"Not you only," added Bernadette. "The lady wishes to see *many* people here at Massabielle."

And soon people would oblige. When the curious villagers of Lourdes found out that Bernadette intended to go to Massabielle every day for fifteen days, many of them decided that they would go along to watch the strange events.

Meanwhile, Bernadette approached her mother.

"Mama, the lady has asked me to return to Massabielle for fifteen days, and I've promised that I will."

Mrs. Soubirous was upset. She feared a trick of the devil. Only the sincerity in her daughter's dark eyes kept her from forbidding Bernadette to go.

Worriedly she explained the situation to her sister Bernarde, Bernadette's godmother. "What can we do, Bernarde? It's all getting out of hand." Bernarde thought a moment, and then slapped her hand on the wooden table, startling Louise.

"Let's go with her ourselves tomorrow. After we've seen what happens, we'll know what to do."

6

Three More Apparitions

"You should bring something blessed," Aunt Bernarde advised Bernadette as they got ready to leave for the grotto.

"Aunt Lucile has a blessed candle," Bernadette thought out loud. "Would you ask her if I can borrow it."

Bernarde nodded.

The pre-dawn chill of that February 19 caused Bernadette, her mother and Aunt Bernarde to hug their shawls tightly as they headed for Massabielle. Even though it was early, a handful of people had already gathered on the bank of the stream. A murmur arose as they saw the three figures approaching, "Bernadette! It's Bernadette!"

Bernadette knelt and began to pray the rosary, making a beautiful sign of the cross as the lady had shown her. She seemed to be unaware of the people around her. Her mother and godmother knelt nearby and watched as Bernadette's appearance began to change. Her face reflected a mysterious light and peace. "Look at her!" some of the onlookers whispered, "she sees something." Many of them were beginning to believe that the Blessed Virgin herself stood before Bernadette. Their eyes were fixed on the girl's face, transfigured by joy, by love.... No one moved. It was as if a spell had been cast.

Not the least choked with emotion was Louise Soubirous. "My God," she murmured, "please don't take her away!"

Early the next morning Bernadette and her mother set out for the grotto again. This time about thirty people had gathered at Massabielle. The light of their flickering candles and lanterns danced in the shadows of the rocky cliff.

Bernadette paid no attention to the spectators. She was thinking only of the beautiful young lady. She knelt quickly and began her rosary. After a few moments her expression became radiant and she opened her arms wide, like a little child reaching toward her mother. A hush fell over the crowd.

At home later on, Bernadette went about her chores as usual. In catechism class she was called upon by Father Pomian, one of the pastor's assistants. When he asked her some of the catechism questions, Bernadette couldn't answer a single one! She confusedly sat down, but her expression remained calm. Although her ignorance disturbed Father Pomian, her humility aroused his respect.

Six o'clock in the morning of February 21 found Bernadette starting out for the grotto in her Sunday clothes. She met many people on the way and found others waiting at the grotto, about a hundred in all. They packed the space around the grotto right to the river's edge. As usual, Bernadette immediately knelt and began to pray. Soon her face lit up and her eyes seemed fixed to the hollow in the cliff above her.

Meanwhile, a small, but ominous, meeting was taking place among three of the local officials: Mayor Lacadé, Imperial Prosecutor Dutour, and Police Commissioner Jacomet. For several days they had been hearing rumors. Now, having seen that the crowds at Massabielle were increasing, they had decided to put an end to the whole matter before higher authorities shamed them by stepping in themselves. "Bernadette must be questioned this very day," the committee decided. "This foolishness has gone on long enough!"

❖ ❖ ❖

"You there, by the door...stay where you are!"

The parishioners filing out of the church after Vespers that Sunday afternoon looked around in confusion as Constable Callet pushed his way toward Bernadette. He clutched at her hood.

"What do you want?" asked Bernadette calmly.

"You're coming with me to the commissioner's office."

The villagers pressed around Bernadette. "You've no right to take her!" someone shouted. "Let her go home to her poor family."

"Stand back!" commanded Callet, as he led Bernadette away. "I'm only doing my duty."

7

INTERROGATION

Commissioner Jacomet was waiting in his office. He had carefully planned for this interview. Because he thought that Bernadette had been faking, he was plotting to catch her off guard and publicly expose the hoax.

"Come in," the commissioner politely invited when Bernadette appeared in his doorway. "Please have a seat."

After some preliminary questions about her name, age and parents, Jacomet got to the point.

"I'm very interested in what's been going on at the grotto of Massabielle," he said, trying hard to sound sincere. "I'd like to know more about it. I just have a few questions to ask you."

Bernadette nodded and Jacomet began the interrogation. The girl clearly and calmly answered each question without a trace of fear or confusion. Jacomet's pen scribbled furiously across his sheets of paper as Bernadette spoke. After the first round of questions he paused and looked up.

"Who is this lady you spoke of?" he demanded.

"I don't know, sir."

"You said she's beautiful. What do you mean by that? How beautiful is she?"

"More beautiful than anyone else I've ever seen!"

"Well, does she move? Does she speak? Or is she still and silent like the statues in the church?"

"Oh, no! She's alive. She smiles and she talks just like we're talking. She even asked me to come back to the grotto for fifteen days."

"And what did you say?"

"I said I would."

"How do your parents feel about all this?"

"At first they thought I was imagining everything...."

"And they were right! If your lady were a real person, other people would be able to see her too. If she's there, why can't they see her?"

"I don't know. I only know that she's real and alive!"

"Well, I can't stop you from believing in

your imaginary lady. But I do have to draw up a report of this interview. Listen now and see if I've correctly taken down what you've said."

Jacomet continued in a business-like tone, "The lady was nineteen or twenty."

"No!" Bernadette protested. "I said she was only sixteen or seventeen."

"She was wearing a blue dress with a white sash."

"No, sir, just the opposite. Her dress was white and her sash was blue."

And so it went. The interview dragged on with the commissioner "reading" the reverse of everything Bernadette had said and the girl firmly correcting him point by point.

Jacomet was getting nowhere and he knew it. He was having a difficult time controlling his temper. Suddenly his tone changed. "I've let you tell your story," he said icily. "But I know more of it than you think I do. It's a complete hoax, which someone has put you up to."

"I don't understand, sir."

"You don't? Well, let me explain. Somebody, in secret, has told you to say that the Blessed Virgin appears to you at Massabielle—so that people will think you're a saint!"

"It's not true! No one ever told me to say anything like that!"

An hour had already passed. Word had spread that Bernadette had been taken into custody like a common criminal and the crowd outside was becoming violent. Stones began to thud against the door. Voices rose in anger.

Jacomet continued to twist Bernadette's words.

"You've changed everything I've said," Bernadette cried.

"It's what you told me!" Jacomet insisted, his face red with rage.

"No, sir."

"Yes!"

"No!"

"Yes!"

"No!"

Jacomet abruptly stood up. "Confess that this whole story is a lie and promise me you won't go back to that grotto again!" he bellowed.

"I've told you the truth. I can't change it."

"Very well. I'm calling the police. You'll be sent to jail," the commissioner threatened, storming out of the room.

Meanwhile the mob outside had grown angrier. Some people were shouting, "Let her out!" Others were banging on the commissioner's door and shutters. François Soubirous had finally been called and now he timidly arrived on the scene. Someone in the crowd recognized him. "You're her father! Get up there and break down the door, if you're man enough to do it!"

Mr. Soubirous felt himself being pushed to the front of the throng. He found himself before the door of the house as it suddenly flew open. He stood face to face with Jacomet, who was actually relieved to see him. Mr. Soubirous stepped in and the door slammed behind him.

"You've come just in time," Jacomet thundered. "I was about to have you called in. You well know that this deception your daughter is practicing is disturbing the peace of the town. If you don't stop it, if you don't keep her away from that grotto, we'll reserve spaces for you both in our jail!"

"To tell you the truth, sir," Mr. Soubirous replied, "I'm tired of the whole thing myself." He glanced over at Bernadette, then turned again to the commissioner. "Bernadette will not return to Massabielle," he said, "I promise you that."

"See to it," Jacomet insisted. "Now take her home."

8

A Mysterious Force

The next morning, before she left for school, Bernadette's father took her aside. "You will walk straight to school, do you understand?" he said in a stern tone. "I'm forbidding you to go to the grotto." Bernadette sadly nodded. She felt miserable about not being able to keep her promise to the lady.

At school things only got worse. The sisters (whose religious congregation she would one day enter) didn't believe in the apparitions, even though they had never gone to Massabielle to witness the transformation which took place in Bernadette. One sister even considered her a tool of the devil!

Bernadette walked home for lunch as usual, then at one o'clock returned to school. Just as she was about to step through the door, "an irresistible force" turned her right around. Bernadette sped back down the hill and headed for the grotto.

Two policemen who had been assigned

to keep an eye on her quickly closed in. "Where are you going?" they questioned.

"To the grotto," she replied simply. She didn't stop, and they didn't try to stop her. Surrounded by a group of children and followed by the two policemen, Bernadette approached the bank of the stream.

The remnants of the morning's crowd were still there. They had lingered to pray, hoping that the girl would come after all. Without any sign of self-consciousness, Bernadette passed among them and knelt at the familiar spot. She took out her rosary and began to pray. But today she prayed much longer than usual. When she stood up to leave, she looked unhappy. The lady hadn't appeared!

Back at home, Bernadette tried to explain things to her parents. "I just couldn't help it," she confessed. "I didn't want to disobey, but something wouldn't let me go anywhere else. I *had* to go to Massabielle!"

Mrs. Soubirous could see that Bernadette was telling the truth. She turned to her husband. He lowered his eyes and sighed quietly, "All right, Bernadette. All right. You may go to the grotto whenever you wish."

The next day, February 23, the young lady of the grotto kept her appointment.

The crowd swelled, and for the first time several important persons were on hand; one of them was Doctor Dozous, a physician from Lourdes.

During this vision the beautiful young lady taught Bernadette a prayer. The teenager had to repeat it several times until she was sure she had learned it. Later on, she recited it often. But she never revealed the prayer to others. It was meant just for her.

The young lady appeared again on the following day. This time she asked Bernadette to go into the interior of the grotto. Moving from the hollow in the rock above, the lady came down to talk to Bernadette in the larger grotto. The crowd watched in suspense as Bernadette nodded "yes," "no," listened, cried and even laughed. Then something new happened. Bernadette started to move on her knees toward the lady. Next she lowered her head until her face touched the ground. She kissed the soil. As if inspired, many of the onlookers bowed to the earth and kissed it too. Those who were too tightly packed together to bend over, reached down and scooped up dirt in their fingers, raised it to their lips and kissed it.

This was all too much for Bernadette's

aunt, Lucile, who suddenly fainted. Bernadette, who was just about to bow to the ground again, stopped short. "Aunt Lucile," she reprimanded, "it's not good to get all worked up like that!"

By the time Bernadette looked back toward the grotto, the lady was gone. The girl was very disappointed. On the way home she said quietly, "Auntie Lucile, you must not come to the grotto with me anymore."

As usual there were many questions about what the lady had said and done.

"What did she tell you this time, Bernadette?" a school teacher questioned.

"You mean you couldn't hear us talking?" Bernadette asked in amazement. "You were so close to me, I was sure you heard everything."

The teacher shook her head.

"She asked me to do penance and to pray to God so that sinners may be converted."

"But why did you bend your head to the ground?" someone else asked.

"Because the lady asked me to kiss the ground as a penance for people who are sinning. Before I kissed the ground, though, she asked if this action would bother me. The lady is always very respectful toward me. I told her it wouldn't bother me at all," Bernadette explained. "The lady looked so sad when she talked about people sinning against God. It made me sad to see her like that."

9

THE MIRACULOUS SPRING

When Bernadette arrived at Massabielle on Thursday, February 25, three hundred people were already waiting there. As usual, she knelt and prayed. But soon enough she began walking back and forth on her knees, as she had done the previous day. This time, she kept whispering "Penance...penance...penance," as she moved toward and then away from the grotto. At one point, she abruptly stood up. She seemed very confused. The crowd pressed closer. "What's going on?" people whispered as they strained to see.

Bernadette started to walk toward the Gave River. Then she stopped and appeared to listen. Nodding her head, she turned back and approached the left side of the grotto. She looked down at the reddish clay and then back up at the hollow in the rock above her. The expression on her face seemed to be asking, "What am I looking for?"

A few seconds passed. Suddenly Bernadette got down on her hands and knees and began digging in the damp dirt. When she had scooped out a small hole, a trickle of muddy water appeared at its bottom. Cupping her hands, Bernadette tried to drink a few drops but had to spit it out because it was more dirt than water. Again she questioningly looked up at the niche in the rock. Again she began to dig. Three times she dug and three times she tried to drink. But she couldn't bring herself to swallow the mud. Finally, as she dug for the fourth time, more water began to fill the small hole. Bernadette managed to capture some and swallow it. Next she filled her palms with the dirty water and "washed" her face with it. Finally, she plucked some leaves from a nearby wild plant and brought them to her lips.

A wave of uneasiness had swept through the crowd. "Stop her! Stop her!" someone yelled. "The poor girl's gone mad!"

But no one moved. And Bernadette ate the weeds. As she stood and turned to leave the grotto, her face was streaked with red mud. Shocked by what had happened, her Aunt Bernarde ran up to her with a handkerchief, frantically trying to wipe the stains from her face.

Bernadette, meanwhile, paid no attention, but calmly returned to her kneeling

Next she filled her palms with the dirty water and "washed" her face with it.

place where she remained motionless, deep in prayer. The mysterious radiance returned to her face. But there were no murmurs of admiration now. The throng felt only pity.

Later, Bernadette was badgered with questions about what had happened.

"The young lady told me to go drink and wash myself in the spring, and to eat some of the grass I would find there," she simply explained. "But I couldn't find any spring, so I was going to drink from the Gave River. When the lady saw me walking toward the river, she showed me that I should go into the grotto and look there. Since I didn't see any water, I began to scrape the dirt, and there it was. Because it was so dirty, I had to throw the water away three times before I could drink it. The fourth time I dug in the hole, I was able to drink some of the water and wash my face with it."

"But why did the lady have you do all that?" someone asked.

"She didn't tell me."

On the afternoon of that February 25, a few persons who had gone to the grotto noticed a trickle of water coming from the small hole Bernadette had scooped out. They made the hole a little bigger and the water continued to increase. Soon it became clear and clean.

By now, some people were beginning to think that Bernadette was crazy. Yet on the day after the spring was discovered, many who believed in what the girl said went to Massabielle to drink from the tiny stream and wash in it. Someone even suggested that the water might help the sick.

Living in Lourdes at the time was a poor man named Louis Bourriette. His right eye had been blinded some twenty years before in the same mine explosion which had killed his brother Joseph. Bourriette was being treated for his pain, but the doctors had told him his sight could never be restored.

When Bourriette learned of the strange spring at Massabielle, he called his daughter and asked for some of its water. She brought it, and the miner made the sign of the cross. Then he began to bathe his injured eye. Suddenly he cried out, "I can see!"

He and his wife and daughter could hardly believe what was happening. Yet, as Bourriette continued to pour the water over his eye, his vision grew better and better!

Eagerly, the miner set out to find Doctor Dozous. He had to tell him what had happened. Meeting Dozous in the public square, he shouted, "I'm cured!"

"It can't be," retorted the doctor. "You're incurable. That medicine I gave you was only to deaden the pain."

"Oh, you're not the one who cured me!" Bourriette corrected. "It was the lady of the grotto!"

Dozous looked at him and shrugged. But then, as his patient kept insisting upon the cure, the doctor pulled out a slip of paper and swiftly wrote a few words on it. Covering Bourriette's left eye with his hand, Dozous held the paper in front of him.

"If you can read this, I'll believe you," he said in exasperation.

Without hesitation the miner read back to him, "Bourriette has an incurable injury and will never recover!"

10
ANOTHER SUMMONS

On the evening of February 25, a loud knock shook the door of the Soubirous home. Mrs. Soubirous answered it. She was shocked to find a policeman standing there.

"I've been sent by the Imperial Prosecutor," he announced. "Bernadette Soubirous is to be at his house at six o'clock this evening."

Mrs. Soubirous panicked. It was market day and her husband was away in the next town. She rushed to the stone quarry to get their cousin André Sajous.

At six o'clock André, Mrs. Soubirous and Bernadette, dressed in their best clothes, rang the prosecutor's doorbell. A maid answered and returned with Prosecutor Dutour.

He eyed André curiously. "Are you the girl's father?"

"No, sir, just a relative. I own the house where she lives."

"Well, you may wait out here. Bernadette and Mrs. Soubirous, please come with me."

Prosecutor Dutour, looking very official in the full uniform of his rank, led them into a large room. Seating himself beneath a gigantic portrait of Napoleon III, he didn't bother to invite Bernadette or her mother to be seated themselves. Like Commissioner Jacomet before him, Dutour had a plan. He began to question Bernadette in a friendly tone about her intention to return to Massabielle.

"I've promised the young lady that I will return for another twelve days," Bernadette answered firmly.

"Ah, but your lady is not real," Dutour smiled with a wave of his hand.

"I'm sure I'm not mistaken, sir," Bernadette replied, "she's come to the grotto many times and has spoken with me."

The prosecutor tried another tactic. "Even the sisters under whom you study say all these things are products of your imagination."

"If they had seen what I've seen, they would believe too," Bernadette shot back.

Again Bernadette had to describe the apparitions in detail. Dutour wrote everything down and then began to read it back to her. As Jacomet had done, the prosecutor "read" things Bernadette hadn't said. She corrected him every time.

"But you said this," Dutour kept asserting.

"No, sir. I didn't."

The prosecutor then insisted that what he was reading back to Bernadette did not match Commissioner Jacomet's report. Bernadette held her ground: "Commissioner Jacomet wrote that paper. If it has mistakes on it, he made them."

After about two hours Dutour stood up. "I'm going to call Jacomet and his officers to take you to jail!"

At that point, Mrs. Soubirous, who like Bernadette had been standing the whole time, began to cry. Bernadette leaned closer to her and whispered, "Why are you crying, Mama? Can you believe that they'll put us in jail when we haven't done anything wrong?"

Dutour pointed to the chairs behind them. "You might as well take a chair," he said scornfully, "until Jacomet arrives."

Mrs. Soubirous immediately dropped into a chair. Bernadette, instead, angry at the way the prosecutor had spoken to her mother, pushed the chair away and sat on the floor. (Years later she would regretfully look back on this action, saying, "How fresh I was!")

In the meantime, André Sajous had told some of his friends what was happening. A crowd had gathered outside, and angry feet were kicking the door. "Let them out!" some men were shouting. They were beginning to sound dangerous. Dutour's tone suddenly softened, "Will you promise not to return to Massabielle, Bernadette?"

"No, sir. I will not promise."

There was an uneasy moment of silence.

"Well then, we'll take up this case again tomorrow, when the commissioner is free," muttered Dutour. "For now, you may go home."

11
The Request

The crowds flocking to the grotto continued to grow day by day. On February 26, the young lady did not appear and Bernadette went away sad. *What have I done to disappoint her?* she asked herself over and over again. *What have I done?*

On February 27 and 28 the lady came as usual and Bernadette repeated her acts of penance, bending low, kissing the ground and washing at the spring.

As she was coming out of Mass on the 28th, Bernadette was abruptly intercepted by Inspector Latapie, the town official in charge of springs and fountains. He whisked her off to another interrogation—this time before the local judge. "Hang on tightly," Bernadette joked as they hurried along, "or I might get away!"

The judge glared down at her from behind his desk. "Why do you keep running off to the grotto?" he barked. "Who's behind this story? If you're not careful, you're going to end up in prison!"

Bernadette wasn't at all impressed by his threat.

"I'm quick," she retorted. "You may put me in jail, but make sure it's a strong one, and well-locked or I'll escape!"

"Stop joking!" the judge roared. "I want you to promise not to return to the grotto or I really will send you to jail!"

"But I *won't* promise not to go there!"

"Then I'll throw you in prison!"

Just at that moment the superior of the sisters at Bernadette's school burst into the room. She was crying. "I beg you, sir, set the girl free!"

The annoyed judge turned to Latapie. "Let her go!" he ordered. "What can you do in a case like this?"

As Bernadette left with the sister, she was saying, "I want to keep going to the grotto until Thursday. That will be the last of the fifteen days."

The twelfth apparition at Massabielle took place on Monday, March 1. On the following day, March 2, over 1,600 people had jammed the area around the grotto by the time Bernadette arrived. Some had been there since midnight. Bernadette paid no attention to the excited crowd. Kneeling on the rock, she made a sign of the cross, and had already begun the rosary when the lady appeared to her. From the movement of Bernadette's lips, the crowd could tell that a conversation was going on between the lady and the teenager.

Toward the end of the vision, the lady seemed to be pondering something. After a few moments she said to Bernadette, "Go and tell the priests that I desire to have a chapel built here and that people are to come here in procession."

Soon the light around her began to fade and Bernadette could no longer see the beautiful lady. As she stood to leave, the girl was immediately hemmed in by the crowd.

"What did she tell you?"

"Is it a secret?"

"You can tell us, Bernadette!"

"The lady said I should tell the priests that people are to come here in procession," Bernadette said quietly. "I must go now."

Bernadette hurried to find her confessor, Father Pomian. She repeated to him all that the lady had said. Father Pomian listened kindly, but what could he do? "Bernadette," he said gently, "you'll have to tell all of this to Father Peyramale. He's the pastor. He'll know what to do."

Of course, Father Peyramale and his assistants knew about the apparitions. How could they help it, when all of Lourdes had been buzzing with the news for two weeks? Father Pomian clearly remembered the advice Bishop Laurence had given the pastor, "It's better not to go to the grotto. If these happenings are from God, he will let you know what to do at the right time."

Father Pomian ran his fingers nervously through his hair as Bernadette turned to leave. He hoped the pastor would know what to do. He really did.

12

THE CHAPEL AND THE PASTOR

Father Peyramale was a big man, with broad shoulders, large hands and rugged features. Although he appeared stern and severe, his gruff exterior hid a kind and gentle heart.

Of all the people Bernadette had to face, the pastor was the one she was most afraid of. *It would be better not to go alone*, she thought. She was very relieved when her aunts, Bernarde and Basile, agreed to accompany her to the rectory.

Father Peyramale was striding up and down in the garden when the three visitors arrived. He stared down at Bernadette. "Are you the one who goes to the grotto?" he asked roughly.

"Yes, Father," Bernadette answered quietly.

"Come with me," he ordered, leading the way into the house.

The pastor sat beneath a big crucifix, while Bernadette and her aunts remained standing. The aunts posted themselves against the wall, trying to keep as far away as possible from the priest.

"So you say you see the Blessed Virgin?" he began abruptly.

Bernadette could feel her face getting hot. She had to force herself to answer. "I never said the lady was the Blessed Virgin, Father."

"Then who is she?" the pastor thundered. "Is she from Lourdes? Do you know her?"

"No, she's not from Lourdes, Father, and I don't know her. She's not like other ladies."

"What do you mean?" he demanded.

"I mean that she's more beautiful than anyone could ever imagine! And she gave me a message for you."

The priest's bushy eyebrows shot up in surprise.

"The lady asked me to tell the priests that she would like processions to come to the grotto," Bernadette said all in one breath.

Father Peyramale stood up. He seemed to grow huger. "A procession!" he roared. "This is really too much! Your lady has sent you to the wrong person. Doesn't she know that only a bishop can order processions?

She should have sent you to the Bishop of Tarbes, not me." He started to pace back and forth. "And when did she say she wanted this procession?"

Father Peyramale's anger was beginning to shake Bernadette. For once, she stumbled. "I, I don't know," she timidly admitted. "She just said that she wants it sometime. If I understood well, she didn't mean right away."

The pastor had had enough. Glaring at Bernadette's trembling aunts, he shouted, "Take the girl home and keep her there! This scandal has to stop!"

Bowing humbly, Bernadette and her aunts backed out the door. Aunt Bernarde immediately ran home. Aunt Basile was in tears. After they had only walked a short distance, Bernadette turned to Basile. "Auntie, we have to go back...I forgot to tell him something...something important!"

"You won't get me in there again!" Basile fumed. "Never again!"

When she arrived home, Bernadette tried to convince her parents to go back to the rectory with her, but they also refused. Then one of the neighbors, Dominiquette Cazenave stopped in. "What did the lady say this morning?" she questioned.

"To tell the priests to have a chapel built and to have processions come to the grotto," Bernadette said, shaking her head in frustration. "But I forgot to tell Father Peyramale about the chapel. Now I have to go back. Will you come with me, Dominiquette? Everyone else is afraid to."

"I'll come Bernadette," the woman answered. "I know how to handle the pastor."

Dominiquette made an appointment with Father Peyramale for that same evening. At seven o'clock she and Bernadette arrived at the big rectory. This time there were four priests waiting in the candlelit parlor—Father Peyramale, his two assistants, Fathers Pène and Serres, and Father Pomian, the chaplain at Bernadette's school. Bernadette's heart was pounding wildly. She hoped she'd be able to speak.

"Sit down, Bernadette," Father Peyramale said coolly, pointing to a huge armchair.

Bernadette obeyed. But the tension was just too much for her. She immediately jumped up again and blurted out, "The lady also told me to tell you to have a chapel built at Massabielle!"

"A chapel?" the pastor boomed. "Besides the procession? Are you sure?"

"Yes, I'm sure, Father!"

"The lady also told me to tell you to have a chapel built at Massabielle!"

"What's this lady's name?"

"I don't know."

"Well, you'll have to ask her," Father Peyramale fired back. "Tell her that the pastor of Lourdes does not deal with people whom he does not know. Tell her I need to know her name."

The other three priests next took turns asking Bernadette questions. She was relieved when the session finally ended. Back out on the dark street, she squeezed the neighbor lady's arm. "Thank you for coming with me, Dominiquette. I'm happy now that I've run my errand for the young lady."

"Don't forget to ask the lady her name the next time you see her," Dominiquette cautioned. "Remember, the pastor won't build the chapel unless she tells him her name."

Bernadette turned serious. "I hope I can remember to ask her. I must remember!"

❖ ❖ ❖

On Wednesday, March 3, Bernadette, accompanied by her mother and father, arrived at the grotto around seven o'clock in the morning. But the lady didn't appear.

After some time, the disappointed throng of nearly 3,000 people began to break up and go home.

Bernadette left, too, but returned later that day with her cousin, André Sajous. This time there were only about 100 curious onlookers. The beautiful lady came. She again made her request for a chapel. And Bernadette asked her important question, "What is your name? The pastor would like to know." The young lady only smiled.

That night found Bernadette at the rectory again. Father Peyramale wasn't happy to see her.

"Father, I saw the lady today and she still wants her chapel," Bernadette said quietly.

"And what about my question?" the priest demanded. "Did you ask her her name?"

"Yes. The lady didn't answer me. She only smiled."

"She's making a fool of you!" the pastor yelled. Then he grew strangely silent, his right hand stroking his chin. "All right," he announced, "if the lady wants a chapel, she must give us a sign. I've heard that she stands on top of a rosebush at the grotto."

Bernadette nodded.

"Well, then, ask her, from me, to make

that bush bloom, all of a sudden, in front of many witnesses. If she does that, we'll have her chapel built."

The following day was March 4, the last of the fifteen days during which Bernadette had promised to visit the grotto. That morning, the largest crowd yet had thronged to Massabielle. People lined both sides of the Gave River and crammed the area around the grotto. Many had been waiting there all night. Some were expecting a miracle.

During the apparition the crowd watched Bernadette's face register alternate joy and sadness—joy whenever the lady smiled, and sadness whenever she asked her to pray for sinners. After the lady had disappeared, Bernadette continued to gaze toward the hollow in the rock. Would she ever see the beautiful young lady again?

Bernadette spent the afternoon trying to hide at her cousin André's house. But the people discovered her and a continuous stream of visitors poured in, pushing and shoving, kissing her hand, embracing her and touching all sorts of objects to her. Bernadette tried to escape, but it was useless; they were everywhere.

"Please, lock the door!" Bernadette begged that night. Although she was happy that she had been able to keep her promise and visit the lady at the grotto for fifteen days, Bernadette was now physically exhausted. She needed to be left alone. She needed to rest.

Meanwhile, the rosebush at the grotto had not bloomed.

Bernadette's mother moaned quietly, "How will all this end?"

13
Annunciation Day

In the middle of the night of March 24, the vigil of the Annunciation, Bernadette awoke, feeling a very strong urge to go to Massabielle. She got up before dawn and told her parents what had happened. "If you must go, your father and I will come with you," Mrs. Soubirous decided.

The sun was creeping toward the horizon when the three arrived at the grotto. They were surprised to see a crowd. About 100 people had gathered, hoping that the lady would come on this Feast of the Annunciation.

Bernadette knelt down. She saw that the hollow in the rock was already glowing with light. Calm and smiling, the beautiful young lady was there, looking down on the people with love. Bernadette begged pardon for being late, but the lady indicated there was no need to apologize.

As Bernadette watched and prayed, one thought kept coming back to her, *"I must find out her name. I don't want to annoy her, but I must ask again—for Father Peyramale."*

"My Lady," Bernadette ventured, "will you please be so kind as to tell me your name?"

The lady only smiled. But Bernadette was determined. She asked again. The lady smiled again. This happened three times. At Bernadette's fourth try, a change came over the young lady. Her face became serious. She seemed to be praying. Then, slipping her rosary over her right arm, she stretched out both arms toward the earth. It was a gesture which made her look just like the image on the miraculous medal. Next she raised and folded her hands, looking up toward heaven. "I am the Immaculate Conception," the lady said. And then she was gone.

What did this strange name mean? Bernadette had no idea. All she knew was that she had to remember it and tell it to the pastor. She headed straight for the rectory, repeating over and over again, *I am the Immaculate Conception.... I am the Immaculate Conception...."*

Finally arriving, Bernadette pushed open the door to the priests' house and walked straight up to Father Peyramale. "I am the Immaculate Conception!" she practically shouted.

The pastor's red face grew pale. Before he could respond, Bernadette continued excitedly, "This is what the lady told me today when I asked her her name: 'I am the Immaculate Conception.'"

"Have you ever heard these words before?"

"No, never, Father."

"Do you know what they mean?"

"No, Father."

"How can you talk like this if you don't even understand what you're saying?" the priest demanded.

"I just kept repeating the words over and over as I ran to tell you, Father," Bernadette said simply.

Father Peyramale was stunned. Now he understood that the young lady of the grotto really was the Blessed Virgin Mary! There was no longer any need for the rosebush to bloom. He had his sign. A deep joy welled up within him and he felt his eyes filling with tears. He turned quickly to hide his feelings from Bernadette. "All right, go home now," he said in a low, shaky voice.

Bernadette didn't understand what was

going on. *Why did Father Peyramale sound as if he were going to cry? What did the lady's strange name mean?* She had to find out.

❖   ❖   ❖

"Tell us what the lady said this morning," begged Emmanuélite as Bernadette took a seat between Emmanuélite and her brother in the Estrade family's home that afternoon.

"I asked the young lady her name," Bernadette explained, "just as Father Peyramale told me to, and this is what happened...."

Bernadette jumped up and began to act out the lady's motions, stretching out her hands, joining them together and raising her eyes toward heaven. "After she did these things," Bernadette concluded, "the lady told me, 'I am the Immaculate Conception.' But I still don't understand what these words mean. Do you?"

Emmanuélite felt a chill run down her spine. She looked at her brother. There were tears in his eyes. Both remembered that four years earlier, Pope Pius IX had solemnly declared it a truth of faith that Mary, the most holy mother of Jesus, was conceived without original sin. And now the Immaculate Lady of Massabielle had come to confirm that wonderful truth on the anniversary of the Annunciation—the greatest day in her life!

"Bernadette," Emmanuélite whispered in awe, "those words mean that the beautiful lady you've seen is the Blessed Virgin Mary!"

14
A Temporary Farewell

On Tuesday, April 7, the Blessed Virgin appeared to Bernadette again, repeating her request that a chapel be built at Massabielle.

A large crowd of onlookers was present, among them Doctor Dozous. His was a scientific mind, which demanded proof. He was opposed to miracles as a matter of principle. On that day the skeptical doctor was in for a great surprise....

Bernadette was praying her rosary with great fervor. The beads were in her partly-open left hand, a lighted candle in her right. She began to move toward the grotto on her knees, then suddenly stopped. When she did so, her right hand came beneath her left. While Bernadette continued to pray, Doctor Dozous saw that the candle flame was passing between the fingers of her left hand! Fanned by a strong current of air, it flared up and licked at her skin. Yet the kneeling girl showed no sign of pain and, what was more astonishing to the physician, her fingers didn't seem to be blackening at all!

*The candle flame was passing
between the fingers of her left hand!*

The amazed doctor urged bystanders not to disturb Bernadette. He took out his pocket watch and watched the phenomenon for fifteen minutes, until she changed position.

After the vision was over, the doctor asked Bernadette to show him her left hand. Puzzled, she held it out. He examined it closely, but found no place where the flesh had been scorched. To complete the experiment, the doctor asked a bystander to relight the candle and hand it to him. But when he brought the flame very close to Bernadette's hand, she quickly pulled it back.

"You're burning me!" she exclaimed.

From that day on Doctor Dozous believed that Bernadette did see something at the grotto.

Three months later, on the Feast of Our Lady of Mount Carmel, the Lady appeared for the last time.

Bernadette was in the parish church, attending Vespers, when she heard an inner voice calling her to the grotto. She joyfully turned to her Aunt Lucile, who was nearby, and asked her to come along.

They neared Massabielle at about eight o'clock in the evening. Because the civil authorities were still hostile and had erected a tall fence around the grotto, Bernadette and her aunt knelt on the opposite side of the Gave River, facing the niche. A few other people were scattered here and there praying.

Soon Bernadette's expression brightened. She was gazing at the Lady, who smiled in greeting and seemed more beautiful than ever. The Lady looked lovingly at Bernadette for a long time. Then she disappeared.

"What did she say?" someone eagerly asked as Bernadette got up to leave.

"Nothing," Bernadette happily sighed.

Bernadette had seen the Blessed Virgin for the last time on this earth. A very special period of her life had ended in the peace of that summer evening.

From now on, Bernadette would retire into the shadows. In the depths of her soul she was aware of her nothingness. She would have considered it a sin to say that she had deserved the honor which she had received.

One day she explained, "The Holy Virgin made use of me because she knew I was the most ignorant; had she found someone more ignorant than I, she would have preferred that person to me."

While Bernadette decreased, the splendor of Lourdes with its beautiful Lady increased, until it became to all the world a blazing sun of faith, hope and love. On July 28, a few days after the last apparition, Bishop Laurence of Tarbes issued a letter to the priests and people of his diocese. In it he announced that he was forming a commission to investigate the unusual events which had taken place at Lourdes.

But it was not until January of 1862 that the bishop sent out a special pastoral letter about the apparitions. It ended with these words: "We judge that the Immaculate Mary, Mother of God, truly appeared to Bernadette Soubirous on February eleventh, 1858, and in the days following, for eighteen times, in the grotto of Massabielle, near the city of Lourdes, and that these apparitions have all the indications of truth and that the faithful may believe in them."

15
DECISION

Dominiquette kicked up little clouds of dust as she walked down the dirt road. She had an idea, a good one, she thought, but she needed to discuss it with Father Peyramale.

At the rectory, Dominiquette reminded the pastor of the poverty and hardships of the Soubirous family. "Bernadette should go to live with the sisters," Dominiquette concluded.

The priest thoughtfully stroked his chin. "I've been thinking the same thing myself," he finally said. "She could get her schooling there as well as room and board. I'll talk to Mother Ursule about it."

Not long after, Bernadette went to live at the local convent of the Sisters of Charity of Nevers, the same sisters who had taught her in school. She did housework for them. One day the bishop of Nevers, who was also Superior General of the sisters, came for his usual visit. He found Bernadette in the kitchen busily cleaning vegetables. Struck by her simplicity and goodness, he decided to speak with her.

That evening the bishop asked Bernadette to tell him about the apparitions. Her straightforwardness made a great impression upon him.

"And now," asked the bishop, "what will you do?"

"I would like to stay here with the sisters, to pray and to work as their maid."

"But it's not possible for you to stay in the convent for good, unless you make vows like the sisters."

Bernadette's face clouded.

"Have you ever thought of becoming a sister yourself?" the bishop prodded.

A smile lit Bernadette's face. Then, just as quickly, it disappeared. "But how could I ever become a sister?" she asked. "I'm poor and ignorant. I'm good for nothing...."

The kind bishop leaned forward in his chair. "Well, this morning I saw that you are very good in the kitchen," he replied. "As for the expenses, we could make an exception...."

Bernadette's heart was beating wildly. "I'll think it over, Your Excellency. I haven't decided yet."

Within a year, Bernadette, now twenty-two years old, had made up her mind. She wanted to give her entire life to Jesus as a sister. She asked to join the Sisters of Charity of Nevers and was accepted into the congregation.

On the day before she left Lourdes for Nevers, Bernadette made one last visit to the grotto at Massabielle. She remained there a long time, remembering and praying. She kissed the rock and the earth as if she wanted to leave the impression of her soul in the beloved spot that she would never see again.

The next morning, wearing a blue dress someone had given her and carrying a canvas bag, Bernadette went to say good-bye to her family. Everyone was sobbing as they hugged her. Only Bernadette managed not to cry. She knew that the city of Nevers was far from her home. She knew that she would miss her family and friends very much. But she was at peace. Mary had shown her how much God loves us and how very close he is to each of us. Bernadette smiled. She knew she would never be alone.

The rumble of the carriage wheels came closer and closer. It was time to go. There were a few empty seats in the coach and Toinette, Aunt Bernarde and one of the local sisters climbed in for the ride to the train station. "Good-bye, good-bye!" Bernadette called as they pulled away.

It was the beginning of a whole new life.

16

STILL POOR AND SMALL

In the eyes of many people, Bernadette was small and unimportant. (She was also actually only four feet seven inches tall!) If it weren't for the fact that God had given her the privilege of seeing his Mother, she could have disappeared from Lourdes without anyone ever noticing.

But God sees things differently. He looks at the heart. And the Lord was very pleased with Bernadette's humble and loving heart. Convent life would bring her new opportunities to keep small and humble....

The superior looked up distractedly at the dark-eyed young woman standing before her desk. "Are you the postulant who just came in from Lourdes?"

"Yes, Reverend Mother."

"What is your name?"

"Bernadette Soubirous."

"What are you able to do?"

"Nothing important, Reverend Mother."

"But then what do you wish us to do with you?"

Bernadette didn't answer. She didn't know what to say!

The superior continued, "Who recommended you to our congregation?"

"The Bishop of Nevers."

At that point the sister threw open her arms in a gesture of despair. "Oh, that dear and holy man, he's always doing something like this! Come, then, to the refectory, and have supper with the sisters from Lourdes. Tomorrow morning, if you are not too tired, you will go to the kitchen to help wash the pots."

That sounded fine to Bernadette!

The next day she washed pots, scrubbed the floor, kneaded bread, and accepted the most humble duties with a smile.

Of course, she still felt homesick. Not long afterwards she wrote to the sisters at Lourdes: "Leonie (another postulant) and I 'bathed' Sunday with our tears. The good sisters encouraged us by saying that this was a sign of a true vocation. But," she continued, "I assure you that the sacrifice would be much worse if we had to leave this place. We feel that this is the house of God."

Bernadette remained as humble, simple and cheerful as she had been at Lourdes. She spread joy wherever she went.

"Is it all right to jump rope here?" she asked a few days after she arrived at the convent. "I've always liked to turn the rope for the others!"

One day Bernadette was in the garden when a sister from one of the other convents came up. "I haven't yet had the good fortune of meeting Bernadette," the visiting sister said, "Where is she? I'd like so much to see her!"

At these words, Bernadette smiled and exclaimed, "But she's here!..."

Taking it as a joke, the other waved her hand in the air and asked, "What do you mean? Is this all there is to Bernadette? Is there nothing more?"

Spontaneously and graciously, Bernadette held out her hand and said with a smile, "Yes, sister, there's nothing more than this!"

Because of her humility, Bernadette always shunned the parlor and avoided meeting visitors. One day a gentleman presented himself at the convent's front door just as Bernadette was passing by. "Sister," he requested, "please be so kind as to call Bernadette here just for a moment."

The little sister smiled. "Bernadette? Yes, of course!" and she hurried off as if she were going to find someone.

Several minutes ticked by and there was still no sign of Bernadette. The gentleman approached the portress. "Isn't it possible to see Bernadette?" he asked.

The sister smiled back in surprise. "Bernadette? But you were speaking with her, and the way she escaped from you, you shouldn't even hope to see her again!"

When she began her novitiate, a time of special study of the religious vows and of the Rule of her congregation, Bernadette received the habit of the Sisters of Nevers and a new name—Sister Marie Bernarde. During recreation periods, she was anything but quiet. She liked to talk, laugh, and run with her companions. Many times she sang some of the songs of the Pyrenees region in her dialect, and really enjoyed it when others couldn't understand the words. But when the bell rang to announce the end of recreation, she immediately stopped whatever she was doing and turned her thoughts back to God.

The time for profession of vows came. All the newly-professed sisters received letters assigning them to their convents and duties—all except Bernadette.

"What about Sister Marie Bernarde?" asked the Bishop of Nevers.

"Your Excellency," replied the superior, "we really have a difficulty here; she's good at very little."

"What will she do then?"

The superior thought for a moment. "Maybe she could be assigned, as a favor, to help the sister in the infirmary."

Bernadette accepted both the humiliation and the task with joy. "I'm like a broom," she remarked once. "What do you do with a broom? You use it and put it back in its place, behind the door. That is my case, too, for the Blessed Mother used me and put me in a corner. That's where I belong, and I'm happy to be there."

In the infirmary, in the position she had been given "as a favor," the goodness of the young sister became more and more obvious. Bernadette was generous, patient, attentive, capable, full of love toward the sick sisters—but at the same time gentle and firm.

One day, seeing a novice who had come part way out from under the covers in order to read the Office of the Blessed Virgin, Bernadette took the book from her hand, "This fervor is mixed with disobedience," she said with a smile.

Again, to another sick novice who had

gone to Mass without permission, she said, "Do you know what rule you should follow in the infirmary?"

"'What is that, sister?' the novice asked.

"'Go to bed at once,'" replied Bernadette.

After two years, she was given the position of sacristan, a duty she loved very much, since it obliged her to spend many hours in chapel, near the Blessed Sacrament.

But Bernadette's health, which had never been good, was getting much worse. She was attacked by asthma, tumors, rheumatism, tuberculosis, and even a blood disease. She often fainted and was sometimes found unconscious on the sacristy floor.

Soon Bernadette returned to the infirmary—this time as a patient. During that time her mother died suddenly. Several months later her father also passed away. The young sister experienced temptations and doubts. But in spite of her sufferings, she was happy and peaceful. She had opened her heart to love, and it made all the difference in her life. Once she explained, "I am happier on my bed of pain with my crucifix than a queen is on her throne."

In her months of trial, Bernadette remained strong in character and never swerved from the course shown her by the

Immaculate Virgin: to pray and to do penance for sinners.

In a notebook, she wrote:

O Jesus, O Mary, make my only joy be loving you and suffering for sinners.

Jesus alone for my Goal; Jesus alone for my Master; Jesus alone for my Model; Jesus alone for my Guide; Jesus alone for my Joy; Jesus alone for my Riches; Jesus alone my Friend!

The more the old self diminishes, the more the new increases; the more I humble myself, the more I grow in the heart of Jesus, my Spouse. A spouse should follow her Spouse.

In another place, she wrote: *My Jesus, fill my heart so full of love that it will one day break for love of you.*

On April 16, 1879, Bernadette's wish came true. That afternoon, in great pain, she asked to be moved from her bed into an armchair. Clutching her crucifix she whispered, "My God...I love you...with all my heart...with all my soul...with all my strength." A few minutes later, gasping for breath, she pleaded twice, "Holy Mary, Mother of God, pray for me...a poor sinner."

When Bernadette motioned that she was thirsty, the sisters handed her a glass. She then made the sign of the cross as perfectly as the Blessed Virgin had taught her. After

*In great pain, Bernadette asked to be
moved from her bed into an armchair.*

sipping a few drops of the drink, she closed her eyes and leaned gently on the arm of the sister who was beside her. Bernadette had gone home to God and his Mother. She was only thirty-five years old.

On December 8, 1933, the Feast of the Immaculate Conception, Bernadette Soubirous was proclaimed a saint by the Church. Every year, on February 11, we celebrate the Feast of Our Lady of Lourdes, in memory of the Blessed Virgin's apparitions to Saint Bernadette.

Thirty years after her death, Bernadette's body was found to be incorrupt. It now rests in the chapel of the convent of Nevers. Her lips are partly open and seem to be praying a continuous "Hail Mary." Her serene eyes now gaze forever at her beautiful Lady and her Son.

17
LOURDES TODAY

Millions of pilgrims from all over the world continue to visit Lourdes. The young, the elderly, the sick, the healthy, the rich, the poor—all travel there to honor God and his Mother. They come to answer Mary's invitation to renew their baptismal promises. They come to receive spiritual and sometimes even physical healing. Each year about 70,000 sick and physically challenged persons make the pilgrimage. They are accompanied by volunteers, nurses and doctors. Everyone who visits Lourdes experiences new hope.

Pilgrims at Lourdes today continue to express their faith in God. They visit the *grotto* of Massabielle and kiss the rock where Mary appeared. They know and believe that God is the real Rock on which all our lives are built.

Inside the grotto is the *niche* where Mary once stood. This niche now holds a statue of the Blessed Virgin. When Bernadette saw this statue, she said, "In some ways the statue does resemble Mary, but it is not nearly as beautiful."

Today there are many crutches hanging in the grotto. These were left by people who were cured and no longer need them. Nearby is also a box in which visitors can place their prayer intentions.

At the back of the grotto is the *miraculous spring* that Mary directed Bernadette to find. Pilgrims are able to fill bottles with water from the spring. Some people wash with the water or drink it as a sign of their trust in God. Because of this trust, God may allow them to be healed or to receive a special grace they have been praying for.

The water of Lourdes reminds us of life, especially of the new life we receive whenever our sins are forgiven in the sacrament of Reconciliation. In the *Chapel of Reconciliation*, which is across from the grotto, pilgrims are welcome to celebrate God's love and mercy in this wonderful sacrament.

Outside of the grotto, to the right, there are seventeen *baths* containing water from the spring. They were cut into the floor of the huge gray rock in 1954. The water that is piped into the baths from the spring is fresh and cool. It has been tested and shown to be ordinary water. Before a person steps down into the water, he or she is invited to pray. Many people have experienced spiritual or even physical healings from being immersed in this water.

Candles are also brought to the grotto in remembrance of Bernadette who came to meet Mary with a burning candle. The candles remind us that Jesus said, "I am the light of the world." The candles burning before the grotto symbolize the prayers of the people who leave them there.

A beautiful *basilica* (a large church built in a special design) stands over the grotto. This is the "chapel" the Blessed Virgin asked for. The basilica has three floors. The top floor, called the *Upper Basilica*, contains stained glass windows that "tell" the story of Mary's apparitions to Bernadette. The next floor down is called the *Crypt*. This section of the church is set aside for silent adoration of Jesus in the Holy Eucharist. Built under the Crypt is the *Rosary Basilica*. On this floor of the church are fifteen small chapels decorated with mosaics of the mysteries of the rosary.

Near the grotto, are life-size *Stations of the Cross*. Each day groups of pilgrims pray at these Stations, remembering Jesus' sufferings, death and resurrection—the story of our salvation.

Every afternoon Jesus in the Holy Eucharist is carried in *procession* through the rows of sick and disabled people and all who come to pray for healing of body and soul. Every evening there is a candlelight procession. The flickering lights of thousands of candles burning in the night remind everyone present that Jesus rose from the dead and overcame the darkness of sin and death on Easter morning. During the procession special hymns are sung to the Blessed Mother in many different languages. The procession reminds pilgrims that they must go out and bring God's message of love and mercy to everyone they meet, just as Bernadette did.

At Lourdes Mary continues to bless all her children with God's light and life. The message of Lourdes today is the same message Mary first gave to Bernadette: Change your hearts and believe in the Gospel of Jesus. Change your life and believe that God loves you very much!

Prayer

Saint Bernadette, God was very pleased with your humble and loving heart. He gave you the special honor of seeing the Blessed Virgin Mary many times during your lifetime. Thank you for sharing Mary's message with us: "Pray for yourselves and for people who sin against God. Change your hearts and live as Jesus taught you to. Believe that God loves you!"

Help me to put this message into practice, Saint Bernadette. Remind me to pray the rosary as often as I can. I want to ask Mary to bring us all closer to her son Jesus. I want to be a messenger of God's love and mercy to everyone I meet.

Amen.

GLOSSARY

1. **Angelus**—a prayer that reminds us of the **Annunciation** (please see below). It consists of three Hail Marys alternated with three verses. According to custom, it is prayed three times a day: at 6:00 A.M., at noon and at 6:00 P.M.

2. **Annunciation, Feast of the**—the day (usually March 25) on which the Church celebrates: 1.) the Archangel Gabriel's announcement to Mary that God had chosen her to be the Mother of his Son; 2.) Mary's agreement to become the Mother of God's Son, and 3.) the moment in which God the Son, the Second Person of the Blessed Trinity, took a human body and soul in Mary's womb through the power of the Holy Spirit, becoming the God-man, Jesus Christ.

3. **Humble**—lowly or meek; the opposite of being proud. We say that a humble person has the virtue of **humility**.

4. **Immaculate Conception**—the privilege God gave Mary in preserving her from

sin from the very beginning of her existence, since she was to become the Mother of his Son. We celebrate the mystery of Mary's Immaculate Conception every year on December 8.

5. **Incorrupt**—not subject to destruction. When we say Saint Bernadette's body is incorrupt, we mean that God has preserved it from the natural process of deterioration that usually takes place after death.

6. **Infirmary**—a place where the sick are cared for.

7. **Interrogation**—an investigation carried out by questioning.

8. **Miraculous Medal**—the medal Saint Catherine Labouré had made and distributed at the request of the Blessed Mother who appeared to her in Paris, France, in 1830—twenty-eight years before the apparitions at Lourdes. This medal pictures Mary with her hands extended. Rays of light are coming from the hands. Around the image of Mary is printed the prayer, "O Mary, conceived without sin, pray for us who have recourse to you." The miraculous medal honors the mystery of Mary's **Immaculate Conception**.

9. **Mosaics**—pictures made of small pieces of colored stone, glass or tile.

10. **Niche**—a hollowed-out area in a wall or rock.

11. **Novice**—a person in the special period of training that comes before the making of vows in religious life. The novice studies the Rule and experiences the way of life of the religious Order or congregation.

12. **Pilgrims**—persons who travel to a holy place to pray and to feel closer to God. The journey they make is called a **pilgrimage**.

13. **Portress**—in some convents, the name given to the sister who answers the door and greets visitors.

14. **Postulant**—a person taking his or her first steps in religious life; a candidate.

15. **Procession**—a religious event in which people walk together from one place to another in order to publicly honor God, the Blessed Virgin or the saints. Processions may be held indoors or outdoors and usually take place at churches or shrines.

16. **Rosary**—a kind of "Gospel prayer" in which we think about important events in the lives of Jesus and Mary. The rosary is

made up of Our Fathers, Hail Marys and Glorys which we pray while using a special set of beads also called a rosary or "rosary beads."

17. **Sacristan**—a person who takes care of the sacred vessels, vestments and various articles used for the celebration of Mass and other liturgical functions.

18. **Vigil**—the day or evening before a special feast, sometimes celebrated as a preparation for the feast.

19. **Vow**—an important promise freely made to God. The most common vows today are those of poverty, chastity and obedience made by members of religious communities.

Who are the Daughters of St. Paul?

We are Catholic sisters with a mission. Our task is to bring the love of Jesus to everyone like Saint Paul did. You can find us in over 50 countries. Our founder, Blessed James Alberione, showed us how to reach out to the world through the media. That's why we publish books, make movies and apps, record music, broadcast on radio, perform concerts, help people at our bookstores, visit parishes, host JClub book fairs, use social media and the Internet, and pray for all of you.

Visit our Web site at www.pauline.org

Pauline BOOKS & MEDIA

The Daughters of St. Paul operate book and media centers at the following addresses. Visit, call, or write the one nearest you today, or find us at www.paulinestore.org.

California
3908 Sepulveda Blvd, Culver City, CA 90230 — 310-397-8676
935 Brewster Avenue, Redwood City, CA 94063 — 650-369-4230

Florida
145 S.W. 107th Avenue, Miami, FL 33174 — 305-559-6715

Hawaii
1143 Bishop Street, Honolulu, HI 96813 — 808-521-2731

Illinois
172 North Michigan Avenue, Chicago, IL 60601 — 312-346-4228

Louisiana
4403 Veterans Memorial Blvd, Metairie, LA 70006 — 504-887-7631

Massachusetts
885 Providence Hwy, Dedham, MA 02026 — 781-326-5385

Missouri
9804 Watson Road, St. Louis, MO 63126 — 314-965-3512

New York
64 W. 38th Street, New York, NY 10018 — 212-754-1110

South Carolina
243 King Street, Charleston, SC 29401 — 843-577-0175

TEXAS
Currently no book center; for parish exhibits or outreach evangelization, contact: 210-569-0500, or SanAntonio@paulinemedia.com, or P.O. Box 761416, San Antonio, TX 78245

Virginia
1025 King Street, Alexandria, VA 22314 — 703-549-3806

Canada
3022 Dufferin Street, Toronto, ON M6B 3T5 — 416-781-9131